Like our Facebook page
@RiddlesandGiggles

Follow us on Instagram
@RiddlesandGiggles_Official

Questions & Customer Service
hello@riddlesandgiggles.com

Halloween Knock Knock Joke Book for Kids

by Riddles and Giggles™

www.riddlesandgiggles.com

FREE BONUS

Get your FREE book download

*Halloween Jokes &
Would You Rather for Kids*

⊘ Contains a collection of fang-tastic
Halloween Jokes and Would You Rather
Halloween-Themed Questions

⊘ More endless giggles and entertainment for
the whole family.

**Claim your FREE book at
www.riddlesandagiggles.com/halloweer**

Or scan with your phone to get
your free download

TABLE OF CONTENTS

WELCOME

Hi there, Jokester!

Knock-knock jokes are a great way for people to have fun and share laughs together.

Lots of people love to tell knock-knock jokes. Some are very funny. Some are just corny. Other knock-knock jokes make no sense at all. One thing we can agree on about knock-knock jokes is that kids love them!

I hope you are one of those kids because if you want a collection of funny, corny and laugh-out-loud knock-knock jokes, this book is for you!

The *Halloween Knock Knock Joke Book for Kids* is an awesome collection of good, clean fun knock-knock jokes that will make you roll your eyes, snort, giggle, groan and laugh out loud.

You can read this whole book or pick which knock-knock jokes you want to read in any order you want.

You can also enjoy reading the knock-knock jokes on your own, or share the jokes with everyone around you. You can also take turns reading the knock-knock jokes out loud with family and friends.

Use these jokes when trick-or-treating and just maybe you'll get an extra treat or two!

So, grab your Halloween treats and get ready for some funny and corny Halloween knock-knock jokes!

PSST...You can also color in the Halloween pictures and use this book as a coloring book AND a joke book!

TIPS ON HOW TO TELL A KNOCK-KNOCK JOKE

- Practice reading the joke out loud a few times to help you remember it. You may want to practice reading in front of a mirror.

- Find a family member or friend and ask them if they want to hear a knock-knock joke.

- As you tell the joke, remember to say it slowly and clearly so people understand every word.

- Adding a small pause helps to build up suspense and can make the joke even funnier.

- Deliver the final punch line. Remember to say it slowly, then wait for the laughs.

- If you mess up, that's OK. Move on and tell another joke. Remember, everyone loves knock-knock jokes!

1

NAMES

Knock, knock.
Who's there?
Hal.
Hal who?
Hal-oh-ween.

Knock, knock.
Who's there?
Juan.
Juan who?
Juan Eyed Monster.

Knock, knock.
Who's there?
Abbott.
Abbott who?
It's Abbott time for
trick or treating!

Knock, knock.
Who's there?
Arthur.
Arthur who?
Arthur ghosts
out tonight?

Knock, knock.
Who's there?
Aida.
Aida who?
Aida, all the Halloween
chocolates!

Knock, knock.
Who's there?
Hank.
Hank who?
Hankerin' to get stuck in
my Halloween candy.

Knock, knock.
Who's there?
Annie.
Annie who?
Is Annie body going on a
Halloween haunt with me?

Knock, knock.
Who's there?
Autumn.
Autumn who?
You autumn know there's
a ghost behind you.

Knock, knock.
Who's there?
Ben.
Ben who?
I've Ben waiting to eat my
Halloween treats all night.

Knock, knock.
Who's there?
Celeste.
Celeste who?
This is Celeste time I'm
asking for candy.

Knock, knock.
Who's there?
Candy.
Candy who?
Candy see the Halloween
decorations?

Knock, knock.
Who's there?
Luke.
Luke who?
Luke at that big
spider over there.

Knock, knock
Who's there?
Diane.
Diane who?
Diane to see how much
Halloween candy I got.

Knock, knock.
Who's there?
Earl.
Earl who?
Earl be happy when it's
time to trick-or-treat.

Knock, knock.
Who's there?
Donna.
Donna who?
Donna tell me
you're a witch?

Knock, knock.
Who's there?
Howie.
Howie who?
Howie gonna get out
of this graveyard?

Knock, knock.
Who's there?
Dustin.
Dustin who?
Halloween came
Dustin time.

Knock, knock.
Who's there?
Eddie.
Eddie who?
Is Eddie body home?
Trick or treat!

Knock, knock.
Who's there?
Robin.
Robin who?
Robin your Halloween
treat bag.

Knock, knock.
Who's there?
Gladys.
Gladys who?
Glad-ys the night
of lots of candy.

Knock, knock.
Who's there?
Frank Stein.
Frank Stein who?
The Frank N. Stein monster.

Knock, knock.
Who's there?
Gordon.
Gordon who?
Gord'un't you glad
it's Halloween?

Knock, knock.
Who's there?
Hans.
Hans who?
Hans over all the candy.

Knock, knock.
Who's there?
Max.
Max who?
Max me happy when
it's Halloween.

Knock, knock.
Who's there?
Harry.
Harry who?
Harry and run from
the haunted house.

Knock, knock.
Who's there?
Heidi.
Heidi who?
Check for monsters
Heidi under your bed!

Knock, knock.
Who's there?
Hope.
Hope who?
Hope your Halloween
costume is different
than mine.

Knock, knock.
Who's there?
Hyde.
Hyde who?
Hyde and seek, because
I'm going to scare you.

Knock, knock.
Who's there?
Iwanna B.
Iwanna B. who?
Iwanna B., your
ghoul friend.

Knock, knock.
Who's there?
Jack.
Jack who?
Jack-o'-lantern!

Knock, knock.
Who's there?
Juana?
Juana who?
Juana go trick-or-
treating with me?

Knock, knock.
Who's there?
Olive.
Olive who?
Olive Halloween, don't you?

Knock, knock.
Who's there?
Dawn.
Dawn who?
Dawn leave me alone in this haunted house.

Knock, knock.
Who's there?
Philip.
Philip who?
Aren't you going to
Philip my treat bag?

Knock, knock.
Who's there?
Shirley.
Shirley who?
Shirley, you're not eating
all that candy?

Knock, knock.
Who's there?
Tyson.
Tyson who?
Tyson garlic around your
neck to ward off vampires.

Knock, knock.
Who's there?
Ivan.
Ivan who?
Ivan like to dress up like a
zombie on Halloween.

Knock, knock.
Who's there?
Wanda.
Wanda who?
Wanda go visit the
haunted house with me?

Knock, knock.
Who's there?
Howard.
Howard who?
Howard you like to go trick
or treating with me?

Knock, knock.
Who's there?
Justin.
Justin who?
Justin time for the Halloween
costume competition.

Knock, knock.
Who's there?
Al.
Al who?
Al exchange Nerds
for your M&M's.

Knock, knock.
Who's there?
Fozzie.
Fozzie who?
Fozzie tenth time,
trick or treat.

Knock, knock.
Who's there?
Hardy.
Hardy who?
Hardy recognized
you, that's a great
Halloween costume.

Knock, knock.
Who's there?
Imogen.
Imogen who?
Imogen Halloween without
trick-or-treating?

Knock, knock.
Who's there?
Anita.
Anita who?
Anita stop eating so
much Halloween candy.

Knock, knock.
Who's there?
Doris.
Doris who?
Doris locked! Let me in!

Knock, knock.
Who's there?
Omar.
Omar who?
Omar gosh, those
decorations are spooky.

Knock, knock.
Who's there?
Hayden
Hayden who?
Hayden out so the
werewolf doesn't get me.

2

WITCHES & VAMPIRES

Knock, knock.
Who's there?
B. Witching.
B. Witching who?
B. witching you a
happy Halloween.

Knock, knock.
Who's there?
Witches.
Witches who?
Witches your favorite
Halloween movie?

Knock, knock.
Who's there?
I vant.
I vant who?
I vant to suck your blood.

Knock, knock.
Who's there?
Ride a.
Ride a who?
Ride a broomstick with me.

Knock, knock.
Who's there?
Witch one.
Witch one who?
Witch one of you wants to
go first into the graveyard?

Knock, knock.
Who's there?
B. Witch. You.
B. Witch You who?
Halloween's no fun when I can't B. Witch you.

Knock, knock.
Who's there?
Fangs.
Fangs who?
Fangs for the candy.

Knock, knock.
Who's there?
Broom.
Broom who?
The witch's car goes broom-broom.

Knock, knock.
Who's there?
Cauldron.
Cauldron who?
I'm glad you picked up.
I've been cauldron you.

Knock, knock.
Who's there?
Brew.
Brew you?
Brew me a potion,
and I'll tell you.

Knock, knock.
Who's there?
Viper.
Viper who?
Viper your mouth. You've
got chocolate on it

Knock, knock.
Who's there?
Sucker.
Sucker who?
Vampires sure are suckers.

Knock, knock.
Who's there?
Donkeys.
Donkeys who?
Don-keys a vampire,
or they'll bite you.

Knock, knock.
Who's there?
Necks.
Necks who?
I'm a vampire looking
for my necks meal.

Knock, knock.
Who's there?
Count.
Count who?
As a vampire, you can
always Count on me.

Knock, knock.
Who's there?
Light switch.
Light switch who?
Who turned off the
lights? A witch?

Knock, knock.
Who's there?
Spell.
Spell who?
Spell out your Halloween
treat bag, my dearie!

Knock, knock.
Who's there?
Toadstool.
Toadstool who?
The toad stool my
Halloween candy.

Knock, knock.
Who's there?
Witch hat.
Witch hat who?
Witch hat looks best with
my Halloween costume?

Knock, knock.
Who's there?
Dizzy spell.
Dizzy spell who?
Diz-zy put a spell on me?

Knock, knock.
Who's there?
Witches.
Witches who?
Witches the way to
the haunted house?

3

GHOSTS & MONSTERS

Knock, knock.
Who's there?
Boogeyman.
Boogeyman who?
Let's Boogey, man!

Knock, knock.
Who's there?
Just one.
Just one who?
I'm just one of the ghouls.

Knock, knock.
Who's there?
Banshee.
Banshee who?
I banish ye ghosts
and ghoulies.

Knock, knock.
Who's there?
Ghost there.
Ghost there, who?
Halt! Who ghost there?

Knock, knock.
Who's there?
Mummy.
Mummy who?
It's your mummy and deady.

Knock, knock.
Who's there?
Bandages.
Bandages who?
It's band-ages since I've seen you.

Knock, knock.
Who's there?
Creep.
Creep who?
Creep it down. The monsters are sleeping!

Knock, knock.
Who's there?
Creature.
Creature who?
Creat-ure dinner or no candy.

Knock, knock.
Who's there?
Ice cream.
Ice cream who?
I scream at monsters

Knock, knock.
Who's there?
Boot.
Boot who?
Boo't to you, too.

Knock, knock.
Who's there?
Groan.
Groan who?
My, you've groan
into a monster!

Knock, knock.
Who's there?
Harry
Harry who?
Harry monster coming
to get you.

Knock, knock.
Who's there?
Ghost.
Ghost who?
Ghost get in line for the
costume contest.

4

SKELETONS & SKULLS

Knock, knock.
Who's there?
Skeleton.
Skeleton who?
Are you ready for some
skele-fun this Halloween?

Knock, knock.
Who's there?
Skeleton.
Skeleton, who?
Skele-ton of candy.

Knock, knock.
Who's there?
Nobody.
Nobody who?
I have no body to
trick-or-treat with.

Knock, knock.
Who's there?
Ahead.
Ahead who?
I'm just a skull trying
to get a head!

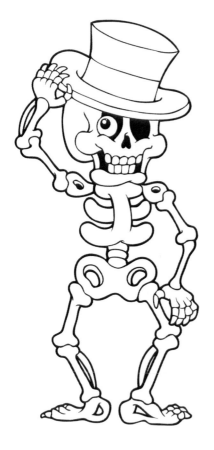

Knock, knock.
Who's there?
No bones.
No bones who?
I'm dead, there's no bones about it!

Knock, knock.
Who's there?
Skeletal.
Skeletal who?
Skele-tell scary
ghost stories.

Knock, knock.
Who's there?
Corpse I.
Corpse I who?
Of corpse I'll go
trick-or-treating!

Knock, knock.
Who's there?
Femur.
Femur who?
I'm sick with a femur.

Knock, knock.
Who's there?
Gutless.
Gutless who?
I may be gutless, but I've
still got backbone.

Knock, knock
Who's there?
Skully.
Skully who?
Skully-ton is bone-shakin' at your door.

Knock, knock.
Who's there?
Tibia.
Tibia who?
I'm a skeleton tibia honest with you.

Knock, knock.
Who's there?
Bone dry.
Bone dry who?
I wish I could cry but my eyes are bone dry!

Knock, knock.
Who's there?
Sherlock.
Sherlock who?
I'm detective Sherlock Bones.

Knock, knock.
Who's there?
You are.
You are who?
You are wanted on
the tele-bone.

Knock, knock.
Who's there?
Backbone.
Backbone who?
Give me back my bones.

Knock, knock.
Who's there?
Spine.
Spine who?
I spine with my little
eye... a skull.

Knock, knock.
Who's there?
Bone.
Bone who?
I was bone to be wild.

Knock, knock.
Who's there?
Tomb marrow.
Tomb marrow who?
Come to the graveyard tomb-
marrow before midnight.

Knock, knock.
Who's there?
Ribbed off.
Ribbed off who?
Someone ribbed
off my bones!

Knock, knock.
Who's there?
Tibea.
Tibea who?
Ti-be-a skeleton
is bone-hard!

Knock, knock.
Who's there?
Fibula.
Fibula who?
I told a little fib-u-la.

Knock, knock.
Who's there?
Bonely.
Bonely who?
It's a bone-ly life
being a skull.

Knock, knock.
Who's there?
Bone.
Bone who?
Bone appetit, it's
time for candy!

5

BATS, CATS, WEREWOLVES & CREEPY CRAWLIES

Knock, knock.
Who's there?
Bats.
Bats who?
Bats the way, uh-huh
uh-huh I like it!

Knock! Knock!
Who's there?
Howl.
Howl who?
Howl you know if you
don't open the door?

Knock, knock.
Who's there?
Honey Bee.
Honey Bee who?
Honey bee careful
trick-or-treating.

Knock, knock.
Who's there?
I bat.
I bat who?
I bat you're scared
of the full moon.

Knock, knock.
Who's there?
Spider.
Spider, who?
I spied-a witch in
the window.

Knock, knock.
Who's there?
Owl.
Owl who?
Owl bet you're excited
for owl-o-ween.

Knock, knock.
Who's there?
Orange.
Orange who?
Orange you glad I'm
not a werewolf?

Knock, knock.
Who's there?
Dead ant.
Dead ant who?
I'm dead ant buried.

Knock, knock.
Who's there?
Bugs.
Bugs who?
Give your ghoul friend
some bugs and hisses.

Knock, knock.
Who's there?
Otter.
Otter who?
You really otter get into
your costume soon.

Knock, knock.
Who's there?
Bee.
Bee who?
Bee-ware of monsters.

Knock, knock.
Who's there?
Werewolf.
Werewolf who?
Werewolf you go when
the moon is full?

Knock, knock.
Who's there?
Toad.
Toad who?
I toad you the house
at the end of the
street was haunted.

Knock, knock.
Who's there?
Snake.
Snake who?
Snake me into the
Halloween party, pleeaase!

Knock, knock.
Who's there?
Buzzard.
Buzzard who?
Buzz-ard doorbell for
treats or tricks.

Knock, knock.
Who's there?
Mice.
Mice who?
Please be mice to other
trick-or-treaters.

BATS, CATS, WEREWOLVES & CREEPY CRAWLIES

Knock, knock.
Who's there?
Gopher.
Gopher who?
Zombies love to go-pher
a walk in the graveyard.

Knock, knock.
Who's there?
Owl.
Owl who?
I wish you a Happy
Owl-oween.

Knock, knock.
Who's there?
Werewolf.
Werewolf who?
Were-wolf you be
on Halloween?

Knock, knock.
Who's there?
Rats.
Rats who?
Rats the last time I ask
you to look after my
Halloween candy.

Knock, knock.
Who's there?
Wolf.
Wolf who?
I'm wolfing forward
to lollipops.

Knock, knock.
Who's there?
Meow.
Meow who?
Cats say Happy
Meow-lo-ween.

Knock, knock.
Who's there?
Daddy Long Legs.
Daddy Long Legs who?
Dad'dys some long
legs on that spider.

Knock, knock.
Who's there?
Wolf spider.
Wolf spider who?
Wolf there be any spiders
in the haunted house?

Knock, knock.
Who's there?
Termite.
Termite who?
Termite be a monster outside.

Knock, knock.
Who's there?
Mantis.
Mantis who?
Man, tis is a great Halloween.

Knock, knock.
Who's there?
Howl.
Howl who?
Howl are you doing
this Halloween?

Knock, knock.
Who's there?
Raven.
Raven who?
I think Halloween is a
raven good time.

Knock, knock.
Who's there?
Crow.
Crow who?
I hope I crow up to
be a wizard.

Knock, knock.
Who's there?
Werewolfing.
Werewolfing who?
We're wolfing down candy!

6

HAUNTED HOUSES & GRAVEYARDS

Knock, knock.
Who's there?
Wooden shoe.
Wooden shoe who?
Wooden shoe like to go
into the haunted house?

Knock, knock.
Who's there?
Armageddon.
Armageddon who?
Armageddon outta
this graveyard.

Knock, knock.
Who's there?
Ooze.
Ooze who?
Ooze there? Hello?
Quick, let's get out of
this haunted house!

Knock, knock.
Who's there?
Tomb many.
Tomb many who?
There are tomb-many
ghosts in this house.

Knock, knock.
Who's there?
Cat-tastrophe!
Cat-tastrophe who?
This spooky house is a
total cat-tastrophe.

Knock, knock.
Who's there?
Lettuce.
Lettuce who?
Lettuce go into the
haunted mansion.

Knock, knock.
Who's there?
Warlock.
Warlock who?
Help! War-locked in
this haunted house!

Knock, knock.
Who's there?
Neverland.
Neverland who?
I'm running from the
cemetery so fast my
feet never-land.

Knock, knock.
Who's there?
Cement.
Cement who?
Ce-ment to explore the
cemetery with you, but
she was too scared.

Knock, knock.
Who's there?
Fright.
Fright who?
Be careful! The ghost
is fright there.

Knock, knock.
Who's there?
Good spirits.
Good spirits who?
The graveyard will put
you in good spirits.

Knock, knock.
Who's there?
Grave.
Grave who?
It's grave to meet you.

Knock, knock.
Who's there?
Dying tomb.
Dying tomb who?
People are dying tomb
get in the graveyard.

Knock, knock.
Who's there?
Morgue.
Morgue who?
At the cemetery, the morgue ghosts the merrier.

Knock, knock.
Who's there?
Diggin' it.
Diggin' it who?
I'm an undertaker and diggin' it is how I roll.

Knock, knock.
Who's there?
Wolf.
Wolf who?
Wolf you like to dance under the full moon?

Knock, knock.
Who's there?
Alaska.
Alaska who?
Alaska mummy for a tomb.

Knock, knock.
Who's there?
Hearse.
Hearse who?
This hearse is haunted!

Knock, knock.
Who's there?
Hugo first.
Hugo first who?
I said hu-go first into the haunted house!

Knock, knock.
Who's there?
Living room.
Living room who?
There are no ghosts in
here. It's the liv-ing room!

Knock, knock.
Who's there?
Chime.
Chime who?
Chime afraid at midnight
on Halloween.

Knock, knock.
Who's there?
Tomb.
Tomb who?
Let me play a great
dance tomb for you.

Knock, knock.
Who's there?
Coffin.
Coffin who?
Eating my Halloween
candy too fast gave
me a coffin' fit.

7

TRICK-OR-TREATING

& HALLOWEEN CELEBRATIONS

Knock, knock.
Who's there?
Goblin.
Goblin who?
I'm goblin up all this candy.

Knock, knock.
Who's there?
Goat.
Goat who?
Goat to the door to
greet our guests for
the Halloween party!

Knock, knock.
Who's there?
Pumpkin.
Pumpkin who?
I'm wishing your Halloween
is pumpkin special.

Knock, knock.
Who's there?
Tinker Bell.
Tinker Bell who?
Tinker Bell isn't working,
try knocking instead.

Knock, knock.
Who's there?
Doughnut.
Doughnut who?
Doughnut look
under the bed!

Knock, knock.
Who's there?
Spook.
Spook who?
Don't spook to me
unless you have candy!

Knock, knock.
Who's there?
Handsome.
Handsome who?
Handsome more
candy to me please.

Knock, knock.
Who's there?
Startled.
Startled who?
Are you ready to get this
Halloween party startled?

Knock, knock.
Who's there?
Gourd-eous.
Gourd-eous who?
These Halloween
decorations are sure
gourd-eous.

Knock, knock.
Who's there?
Eerie.
Eerie who?
This candy is eerie-sistable.

Knock, knock.
Who's there?
Uncandy.
Uncandy who?
You look so much like a
witch, it's un-candy.

Knock, knock.
Who's there?
Voodoo.
Voodoo who?
Voodoo you think is
at the front door?

Knock, knock.
Who's there?
Essen.
Essen who?
Essen it fun to dress
up at Halloween?

Knock, knock.
Who's there?
Getyur.
Getyur who?
Getyur paws off of my
Halloween candy.

Knock, knock.
Who's there?
Carvin'.
Carvin' who?
I'm carvin' up this pumpkin.

Knock, knock.
Who's there?
Police.
Police who?
Police give me
more chocolate.

Knock, knock.
Who's there?
Butter.
Butter who?
You butter look behind
you on Halloween.

Knock, knock.
Who's there?
Norway.
Norway who?
There's Nor-way I'm missing
this Halloween party.

Knock, knock.
Who's there?
Tad.
Tad who?
Tad's the biggest
pumpkin I've ever seen.

Knock, knock.
Who's there?
Gnash.
Gnash who?
Can I gnash you for
some Sweetarts?

Knock, knock.
Who's there?
Horror.
Horror who?
Hor-ror-ay for Halloween.

Knock, knock.
Who's there?
Bats.
Bats who?
Bats the best Halloween
costume.

Knock, knock.
Who's there?
Shriek.
Shriek who?
Trick-or-shriek.

Knock, knock.
Who's there?
Dozen.
Dozen who?
Dozen eating candy
make you happy?

Knock, knock.
Who's there?
Wine.
Wine who?
Wine don't you like my
Halloween costume?

Knock, knock.
Who's there?
Booty.
Booty who?
The Halloween decorations
are boo-tiful.

Knock, knock.
Who's there?
Jacky.
Jacky who?
Jack-y lantern.

Knock, knock.
Who's there?
Shaker.
Shaker who?
Shak-er booty this Halloween.

Knock, knock.
Who's there?
Gummy.
Gummy who?
Gum-me my treat
bag back.

Knock, knock.
Who's there?
Bobbing.
Bobbing who?
Bob-bing, bob-
boo, for apples.

Knock, knock.
Who's there?
Owl.
Owl who?
Owl trade you this
chocolate for a sucker.

Knock, knock.
Who's there?
Halloween candy.
Halloween candy who?
Halloween candy
creeps me happy.

Knock, knock.
Who's there?
Monster Mash.
Monster Mash who?
Monsters mash their
teeth on candy.

Knock, knock.
Who's there?
Halloween!
Halloween who?
Halloween is nearly here.
I can feel it in the scare.

Knock, knock.
Who's there?
Zombie.
Zombie who?
Zom-bie dead on your feet
after trick-or-treating!

Knock, knock.
Who's there?
Fright.
Fright who?
I fright eat too much
candy tonight.

Knock, knock.
Who's there?
Bewitching hour.
Bewitching hour who?
Be-witching hour treat
bags are full by midnight.

Knock, knock.
Who's there?
Goosebump.
Goosebump who?
On Halloween, things
goose bump in the night!

Knock, knock.
Who's there?
Candy.
Candy who?
Candy open the
door any slower?

Knock, knock.
Who's there?
Canoe.
Canoe who?
Canoe please come trick-
or-treating with me?

Knock, knock.
Who's there?
Ice cream
Ice cream who?
Ice cream, you scream, we
all scream on Halloween!

Knock, knock.
Who's there?
Twick.
Twick who?
Twick or tweet, smell
my feet, give me
something good to eat.

BEFORE YOU GO

Did you have fun with those sometimes corny, Halloween knock-knock jokes?

Now that you have gotten the hang of knock-knock jokes, spend some time thinking up some of your own! Create your own jokes thinking of some fun things you like about Halloween.

You can create jokes about witches, ghosts, monsters, zombies, haunted houses and the fun you can have during Halloween such as costumes, parties and not to mention trick-or-treating.

Once you think up your own knock-knock jokes, you can play the game anywhere! It is a great game to play on long road trips, at school or even when you are waiting in line at the grocery store.

Have fun coming up with your own jokes and endless giggles!

WRITE YOUR OWN JOKES!

Have fun coming up with your own jokes and endless giggles!

HALLOWEEN KNOCK KNOCK JOKE BOOK FOR KIDS

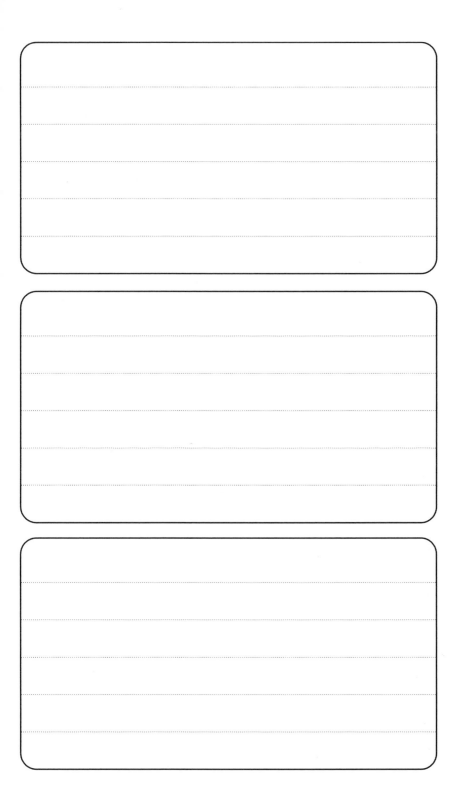

HALLOWEEN KNOCK KNOCK JOKE BOOK FOR KIDS

HALLOWEEN KNOCK KNOCK JOKE BOOK FOR KIDS

HALLOWEEN KNOCK KNOCK JOKE BOOK FOR KIDS

HALLOWEEN KNOCK KNOCK JOKE BOOK FOR KIDS

HALLOWEEN KNOCK KNOCK JOKE BOOK FOR KIDS

HALLOWEEN KNOCK KNOCK JOKE BOOK FOR KIDS

COLLECT THEM ALL!

Halloween
Would You Rather
for Kids

Halloween
Joke Book
for Kids

Halloween
Knock Knock Joke
Book for Kids

www.riddlesandgiggles.com

REFERENCES

18 Haunted House Jokes And Puns To Haunt Your Friends With! (n.d.). Laffgaff.com. https://laffgaff.com/haunted-house-jokes-puns/

Cavoto, E. (2021, June 14). *85 Funny Halloween Puns to Make You Hallo-Scream With Laughter.* The Pioneer Woman. https://www.thepioneerwoman.com/holidays-celebrations/a33298026/halloween-puns/

Chapman, R. (2019, October 8). *47 Puns For Your Halloween Pictures If You Want To Creep It Real.* Elite Daily. https://www.elitedaily.com/life/halloween-puns-for-instagram/2078391

Dubin, A. (2021, June 14). *70 Eerie-Sistable Halloween Puns to Get the Crowd Howling.* Woman's Day; Hearst Media. https://www.womansday.com/life/a36717725/halloween-puns/

Gunner, J. (n.d.). Examples of Puns. https://examples.yourdictionary.com/examples-of-puns.html

Jeon, H. (2021, June 16). *75 Fun Halloween Puns to Creep It Real at Your Spook-tacular Celebration.* Good Housekeeping; Hearst Media. https://www.goodhousekeeping.com/holidays/halloween-ideas/a33001797/halloween-puns/

Kidadl Team. (2020, December 1). *80+ Best Witch Puns And Jokes That Are Wickedly Good* by Kidadl. Kidadl.com. https://kidadl.com/articles/best-witch-puns-and-jokes-that-are-wickedly-good

Kidadl Team. (2020, December 18). *40 Skeleton Puns That Are Rib Breakingly Funny* by Kidadl. Kidadl.com. https://kidadl.com/articles/skeleton-puns-that-are-rib-breakingly-funny

Made in United States
North Haven, CT
25 October 2021